Trade Winds:
Persons, Places, Things

poems by

John F. Sherry, Jr.

Finishing Line Press
Georgetown, Kentucky

Trade Winds:
Persons, Places, Things

Copyright © 2016 by John F. Sherry, Jr.
ISBN 978-1-63534-061-7 First Edition
All rights reserved under International and Pan-American Copyright Conventions.
No part of this book may be reproduced in any manner whatsoever without written permission from the publisher, except in the case of brief quotations embodied in critical articles and reviews.

ACKNOWLEDGMENTS

The author thanks the following sources for permission to reprint these poems: robbing peter, from Four Poems, in *disClosure: A Journal of Social Theory* Volume 24, pp. 71-74, 2014; child in a shopping cart, tantalus, sumptuary law, In Medias Res, from Rack of Want, *Journal of Macromarketing*, 33 (3): 258, 2013; Sanctuary (Black Rock City), Puerto de las Cruceros, Regina Cantata, from Three Poems on Markets and Consumption, *Culture Markets and Consumption* 11 (3): 203-206, 2008; Hump Flute; market music; One Tuna Caught this Day in Diamant, from *Representing Consumers: Voices, Views and Visions*, ed, Barbara Stern, New York: Routledge, 303-305; Krung Thep, Mah Boon Krong, Loy Kratong, from Trivium Siam, CMC: *Consumption, Markets & Culture*, 1 (1): 91-95, 1997; The Price of Martyrdom, from *International Journal of Research in Marketing*, 10 (3): 225; 341, 1993; Unter den Linden, Madison and Mine, from *Public Culture*, 4 (2): 139-140, 1992; Local Custom, from *Anthropology and Humanism Quarterly*, 16 (4), 145-146; 148, 1991.

Publisher: Leah Maines

Editor: Christen Kincaid

Cover Art: Stephanie Wulz

Author Photo: Mark Battrell

Cover Design: Elizabeth Maines

Printed in the USA on acid-free paper.
Order online: www.finishinglinepress.com
   also available on amazon.com

Author inquiries and mail orders:
Finishing Line Press
P. O. Box 1626
Georgetown, Kentucky 40324
U. S. A.

Table of Contents

PERSONS

child in a shopping cart 1
robbing peter..2
tantalus..3
God Willing...4
Consumer Verbatim..5
artisanal inquiry (the philosopher's stoned) 6
sitting in the back of a crowded lecture hall 7
sumptuary law..8
Sanctuary (Black Rock City)..9
Unter Den Linden, Madison and Mine: Meditation
 on a Fragment of the Berlin Wall 10

PLACES

Salvē Minerva...12
Curating Barcelona...13
alley of rogues 14
Beyond Dungiven..15
Fashion Week, Milano 16
Krung Thep 17
Mah Boon Krong...20
Local Custom [Field Journal/Amsterdam Station].................21
Puerto de las Cruceros..22
Regina Cantata...24

THINGS

on first looking into mclellan's things come apart..................26
brand 27
In Medias Res...28
masque 29
One Tuna Caught this Day in Diamant.....................................30
The Price of Martyrdom 31
Loy Krathong 32
Hump Flute 33
market music..34
Hollow Ground..36

PERSONS

child in a shopping cart

bound like Odysseus to the mast,
caressed by soft brand chanting,
wispy filaments of antiphon
responding to her heart song
yaw of yearning,
her ardent earnest
echolalia of longing,
she sways against the buckle
eyes aswivel as she rocks.
resist, her mother whispers,
just sing back,
absorb the stories,
join them to your own,
sing back the lull of buy
each tour of lure,
turn every song
back to its primal hearth
and it is yours.

PERSONS

robbing peter

they argue for hours, carping over coupons
        and rebates dated just before the mortgage,
dunning letters littering a tabled shimmed
        with inserts from *the weekly shopper,*
red ink seeping from each column of the checkbook,
        cracked plastic cover scuffed and scored,
hiding scrimp and kiting, debt demanding
        more than might be wrung from turnip, spun from flax,
until, imagination lapsed, they withdraw, spent.

PERSONS

tantalus

steeped in sweet water rising to his neck,
lush branches brushing softly on his back,
he longs to lap the lake and pluck the fruit,
to feel sweet nectar dribble down his chin.
drooped boughs rock back and dodge his grasp,
the lake recedes each time he stoops to drink.
forever parched and starved he still must strain
to slake and sate, and savor what he can't.
sacrificing sons, devouring daughters
must always end in feasting thus deferred,
with our sad habit halving any hope,
our awful wanting waving in the wind.

PERSONS

God Willing

may you be
almost worldly,
sitting dark in a coffeehouse in Ankara,
heat lightning dancing in the distant hills,
nursing a precise future
traced in aromatic saucer silt
cupped in stained ceramic,
parsed by fortune teller
to the slammed staccato
of okey tile
on sticky table top,
styptic tobacco smoke
a gauze around your eyes,
not yearning for
alternate endings

Consumer Verbatim

Heinz ketchup and French's mustard
always go together.
If you have French's mustard
and Delmonte catsup,
I'm upset.
I don't lose sleep over it,
but they don't go together.
They're mismatched
and disorderly.

I use Bounce fabric softener
and liquid detergent.
I would never use powder—
it doesn't fit in my space.
I would worry
that it was in there,
getting caked up
and taking up space.
Right now, I have liquid fabric
softener on the floor,
instead of Bounce on the dryer,
where it belongs.

You just get used
to seeing things that way.
If I use the other brands,
they stay on the floor.

PERSONS

artisanal inquiry (the philosopher's stoned)

graphite drawing pencils
throw the best first draft.
4b are best or
even 3 will carve
a page with tight
black furrows, dark dust
dancing in the inscribed
lines, smudging in the wake
of trailing fingers
lingering in the trough
of inspired fragments
phrased, then struck through
with brash hash marks
and baroque curlicues
of errant motivated grey-
erasure's not an option,
what's made dare not be
unmade, just realigned—
then phrased again until each word is not
pinned as much as
mashed into the stock,
as a pestle marries matter to the mortar,
powder of my industry
awaiting whispered breath
of anxious inspiration,
last whisked grit of carbon cover,
that reveals what I am making
might transmute lead into gold.

sitting in the back of a crowded lecture hall

the lecturer drones on,
hewing to the script,
siphoning hope out of the room,
relentless in the piling on of detail,
punishing the audience with
earnest plodding effort,
the lecturer drones on,
as Zeno's paradox exacts
an awful toll,
each pulse of digital duration
feeling chiseled on the wall clock,
each minute dragging
ever longer than the last,
a Chinese water torture
of irrelevance,
the echo of the info drip
drives students to their own devices,
the lecturer drones on,
amidst I-M'ing, email
checking, YouTube surfing,
iPod nodding and the shopping
for anything to spring
these confined scholars
from this sapping sell.
The lecturer drones on,
being history,
and I agree
with the stage whisper
of a bailing refugee:
I must uncarcerate
my sorry ass,
the lecturer drones on

PERSONS

sumptuary law

we live above our station as a rule,
the styptic tang of longing on our tongues,
our precious mettle burnished to a brittle film,
our wisdom purled in lazy ruffles
riprapped to restrain our worth
from leeching like diluted wine
unearned, unmerited, uncasked, until
the plainspun fabric of our fine lives frays,
worn shiny from the rub of gorgeous ornament,
until our stores of hoarded spice and silk are sacked,
our gems and jewels, meats and massive headstones sundered
in our rush to draw fresh cards,
the flush of fortune cankering our cheek,
the play of want denied indulged,
like hoarfrost leaving whiskers

Sanctuary (Black Rock City)

Outwaiting a whiteout
    In Medusa's womb
        With dismembered dolls,
    Gilded and garlanded,
Heads on greenglass bottles,
    Arms and legs preserved
        In a Culligan keg.
    Dust drifts on the altar,
On offertory gifts
    Of M&Ms and glow sticks,
        Chianti and acanthus
    On a base blue circle.
Vulval streamers
    Celebrating days
        Whip 'round me while I write.
    The storm abates, then boils
As fast, abates and boils
    Again before it dies,
        The evanescent aura
    Of art outside this art,
Beyond this holy yurt
    And then inside it, too
        Leaves me, only, to
    Imagine and recall
Eroica on the wind.

PERSONS

Unter Den Linden, Madison and Mine: Meditation on a Fragment of the Berlin Wall

It sits there, on the Sony on my desk
Academic, bracketed by books,
Suntory beer, a cast of Peking man,
Flanked by crayon drawings, woodblock prints
Beyond the cathode glow and windowlight
Above the papers and the Post-it notes
That shuffled and reshuffled slow my work.
Still boxed, still pouched, still born upon receipt,
An art effect of unreflective stone;
A piece of rock, a piece of the true wall,
The very cardboard incarnation of
Totemic cant confirming toys are us.

Nowhere there is that doesn't love a mall.
Good neighbors fence for makers
Who still fashion with a hammer and appall.
Dilated, the new takers,
Eyeglasses empty as a butcher's case
Inconsummate, not needy,
Must hear stoned idylls of the marketplace.
Asbestos and graffiti,

Wallpeckers chisel sentiment and rock
The street, the alley flower
Beyond the gate, no triple witching hour
Glass catches grains from any pock.

Cased presentation pieces, segments large
And small, authentic ornamental past,
Brokered relics healing fissured hearts, all
Trailing like a meteor to become
A trophy, a mosaic on the shelves
Of discount houses and dismantled chains.
Astonished by barbarians at our walls
And hesitant to welcome this good buy,
This last grasp margin call philosophy
Of longing that of late restrained them, we
In our glass houses saved by boundary stones
Consume what's left, the customer is right.

PERSONS

For all of that, this unturned stone is mine;
Around this rock I've built my own small shrine:
A wall of mirrors to pacify the urge
For wailing, mending or for writing on,
For tumbling down or tunneling beneath,
A great black wall of ages built to scale,
A threshold god, a fitful monument
To kindergarten hordes who couldn't share
The wealth or burden of a new found world
Of bright and shiny sharp and sterile stuff,
Prima materia worn down to clay,
To all whose labor changes stone to bread

PLACES

Salvē Minerva

quitting the somber site this dreary afternoon
of St. Augustine's reinterred remains,
his bones no older than my own now feel,

measuring in imagination all those switchbacks
from Carthage to Pavia, from black and white to color,

raising my eyes in time to break the spell
and catch a low dull monumental
glint of golden scrotum
(the horse balls of the Regisole await
another gilding by another horde
of errant scholar painters in their cups)

remembering the holy rhetor's guileless wish—
"Master, make me chaste and celibate,
but not quite yet," the prayer is roughly glossed—

wondering if my own door was drawn tight
before the horse had run unbridled through the world

mourning the gelded apples of the son

PLACES

Curating Barcelona

Just off
La Rambla,
Where hordes of
Jocund tourists
Taunting mimes
Give way

To quick
Rivulets of wanderers,
The pulsing cobbled
Capillarity
Of Catalunya,
Stemmed only by displays of
Shop glass and scrawled walls,
Or the smell of market tapas,

Beyond young taggers
Shilling for a
Festival of brands,
Sponsored spray-painting
An aerosol attack on art,

I watched an old man
Fingering the grated walks,
Installing an efficient
Playful comment
On the commons.

Drawing lengths of toilet paper
From a clutch of rolls,
Tying tissue to the bars
And grilles he trudged,
And to itself,

Launching inverted mobiles,
Fantastic paper sculptures
Dancing in the updrafts
Festive as Sagrada Familia,
Serious as Casa Batio,

He never seemed to finish

PLACES

alley of rogues

shaking the carpet from her parapet
each sharp snap sending dirt
and flakes of gritty lint
to flock the neighbor's wet wash
cracking in the stiff breeze
on overloaded lines stretched low
beneath the balcony rail.
she finishes with a flourish,
drapes the rug across her shoulder,
and takes one long last deep drag
before flicking the butt into space,
watching it arc across the narrow alley
to bounce on cobblestones
where it settles with dozens of others
at the crest of the stairs.

PLACES

Beyond Dungiven

starlight
broadcast in stark clusters over hills
behind a misty night so black
you wear it like a wetsuit,
city lights a soft suggestion
somewhere over your right shoulder,
farm houses scattered wildly,
their random glowing panes
flickering on the edge of vision,
roofs luminous
with rain slick slate,
their cracked ceramic chimney pots
glazed with ancient soot,
the dank offing of sheep
like so may ripe bolls splotched in imagination
where Cara soared and Eoghan overreached
they all allowed, that drab allowance
binding dignity to place,
integrity to place
as if lodging it in field stones
turned to cottage walls and fences
could keep you here
forever

PLACES

Fashion Week, Milano

    stalking,
                    watching her cradle mobile to ear,
   gliding the narrow walkway,
                      threading the stylish throng,
     tracking her eloquent free hand
           launching an affable adagio,
   ascending an elegant allargando,
            growing an amiable allegro,
       rising to full on animato,
                cleaving corso with kata,
        throwing ten hands,
           pressing, kihon close to kumite,
        stunning.

PLACES

Krung Thep

In this city of angels
amulet sellers
cellular phones,

saffron boddhisatvas glide
among the throng above the walk,
like marigolds adrift
upon a clotted klong
their stubbled scalps
an almost burnished bronze
of amulet patina,
their sole rejoinder
to a world become
a carnal kindergarten
one again

In this city of angels
amulet sellers
cellular phones,

a young grandmother
braced against unbalanced weight,
stooped below
a bowed yoke
humps her eggs
her melons and her nuts
across a cobbled corridor,
hugs the shadow parsed along
the path of worn umbrellas
tenting vendors in the open air
and marigilded mendicants
with empty bowls,
her eyes alive beneath
the broad straw brim
to every hint
of hunger in the stalls

In this city of angels
amulet sellers
cellular phones,

PLACES

children of Chao Phraya,
houses on the water's edge
on stilts
defy the floating weeds
and polystyrene
that choke the fluid freeway
at their doors
and dive with joyful noise
into the brack,
displacing petrol rainbows
on the ripples of the drink,
bob for blocks of soap
pitched with a mother's eye
toward dampening
the early morning din,
rinse, brush their teeth,
then mount the stairs
and dress
for work

In this city of angels
amulet sellers
cellular phones,

young muay thai oblates,
their rituals lacking grace,
atonal music guiding
their dumb dance,
slap sole against the sacred head
unseating spirit, sense
and will to strive,
the blessing bruise
delivered with the knee
then with the fist
while gamblers sign
the universal gestures
of the trading pits
amidst the building roar,
fingering, hawking snot

PLACES

and smoking hard,
making market, mocking merit,
divided by the action
in the ring
the card and unmade partners
on an upper bench

In this city of angels
amulet sellers
cellular phones,

young girls, clean girls
beautiful girls
becomes the mantra
given to the guest
without the tongue
to order beer and not get laid,
that funds upcountry families
fractured
in the iron mortar
of pestilent advance
who offer up
these sacrificial virgins
to the dark
genius of this place
as fruit or garland
on a spirit house,
whose farming fathers still
must end their days
between the handles
of a taxi

In this city of angels
amulet sellers
cellular phones

PLACES

Mah Boon Krong

urbane silken
        teenage Thais
                surround HDTV
                entranced by the
      loud mouthings of
the wrestlers of the
        World Federation
                amidst the rant and wait
                of shoppers sifting jeans
      and compact discs
enroute to KFC

PLACES

Local Custom [Field Journal/Amsterdam Station]

At last the rain relents.

Sunlight warms the bridge rails
And the smell of sweat and sausages,
Of diesel fumes and cold canals
Is wafted into town on measured gusts.

A ragged band of unwashed foreign boys,
A fluid claque of banter and percussion,
The very occidental tourist becomes

An accidental terrorist
Safeguarded by a bungling host.

Exchanging currency as they embody it,
They mount a raucous randy quest
For guilder bags and golden arches.

As life unfolds, Imbaya Kuna trill
Andean tunes outside the station,
Lilt and shill, accompany hawked tapes,
And dare ethnographers to record

The truth of this Dutch treat.

PLACES

Puerto de las Cruceros

At skyline, on sea rim,
They favor pyramids,
Resolve to mountain
Villages, cresting,
Troughing, drawing close
To manifest as boats,
Bearing Quetzalcoatl's
Cousins, once removed.

They choke the port in numbers,
Each funnel a proud
Palimpsest, each logo
Barely masking a bold
Horn of plenty,
Racked like panpipes on each top deck,
Flying false flags before
The jolly rajas rise.

Disgorged down gangplanks,
Turistas hit the beach,
Dodging beggars, jousting
With indolent vendors
Whose cookie-cutter come-ons
Delay the sack of stalls,
Rude T-shirts, fakelore
Curios, sacral schlock.

How often I have watched
Boat people scrub their hands
With vigor, with disgust,
And pray Purell will
Purify the palm defiled
By accident, by
Local touch, or fingers
Fouled by grazing craftwork.

"Seen one village, seen 'em all,"
Slurred like a mantra
By the sunburned and the slow,

PLACES

In straw hats and sweatsuits
They throng home to Mother,
Their boat, for succor, to embrace
All seven deadlies. Again.

"¡Vaya con Dios!"
Ancient malediction,
Spiel spat with smile and nod,
Hurled after "Meester
Weeskers," after "Harley,"
After "Chica" and the rest,
Wasted in tender wake
And the cries of gulls.

Marooned back in Vandalia.
Tagalog gofer hangtime,
Hand towel origami
And dinner jacket bingo
Relax their grip once more.
New worlds to number
Shimmer on the sea.

PLACES

Regina Cantata

A horde of plastic people
Swaddled, shopping bagged,
Volvate, vermillion,
Stream toward the aunt pharm
As well as just away,
Returning to the source—
No cradle board or stroller
For these regal children.

Memento Mori: American Girl

Post-Columbian
Exposition, Midway
Plaisance in miniature,
Wunderkind in
Wunderkammer playspace,
Exploded home, hearth,
And holdings on display—
Curated, catalogued,
Boxed for your pleasure.

Slice of life in a booth,
Phoned in by experts
Staking Barbie, staving
Off Homies and Bratz,
Culture counters history
And herstory wins—
Asynchronous sorties
Cleave generations.

Bluehair down through towhead
Groom and dress the past
With talk, and talk of talk,
Repairing culture
In the warp of words and
Weft of woman's ways—
Father couched and curbed
Outside, always outside.

Memento Vivere: American Girl Today

PLACES

Valley of the dolls,
Quickened terra cotta
Preppies of Xian,
Dampened once like *moai*
On Rapa Nui,
Now pleasant under glass—
No need to break in
Case insurgency.

Twilight of the idols,
Doppelganger soul mates,
Exotic secret selves,
Curios, fetishes,
Snow clones melting in
The waning warmth of want—
Before choral risers,
Daughters search and dicker.

Flesh of the used gods,
And eyes and hair and clothes,
Memetic parcels
Meted out on tickets,
Collected, surrendered,
Pulsing this playground—
The soft sororal
Systole of shopping.

Like starter dough shared out
Across the households,
Engendered kinship
Energizes girls, as
Mothers and grandmothers
Labor to release
Brandchild from buyosphere
With still more merchandise.

THINGS

on first looking into mclellan's things come apart[1]

o improvised implosive artifice,
to knock the stuffing out of stuff
in such a joyful burst
of perverse engineering,
to celebrate a blowout,
dissembling dandelion mechanics
on brico-lurid bass-o-matic'd breath,
then reclaim every cog and coil,
each bolt and bezel,
strut and spoke and shim,
realigning all in anal complement,
eternal aside, ephemeral together,
the sum of parts just parts
undone, undead,
a hole in imagination
that swallows self and leaves
an anxious aftertaste—
the image overwhelms the word,
I wonder
what you meant to say

---

[1]McClellan, Todd (2013) Things Come Apart, London: Thames and Hudson

brand

so long our hearts
did slaver for astonishment
that now the ritual pang,
so sated by the story glut
that petrifies pretenders to its call,
has atrophied, a dull hull,
like aromatic bitters on the tongue,
like ashes and honey

THINGS

In Medias Res

We find ourselves in the middle of things,
    Thrust into warm middens or spare lairs,
        Left to thumb our way to wisdom
            Bearing stuff sacks full of kit.

We blind ourselves in the middle of things,
    And cauterize a dream of second sight,
        We win no second chance and no sixth sense,
            But hooves of clay and cloying fantasy.

We mind ourselves in the middle of things,
    Juddering like a cart with one bad wheel,
        Condemned to cruise each cramped and crowded aisle
            Till we recall what we've left off the list.

We bind ourselves in the middle of things,
    Gift circuits breaking only to be tripped by trade,
        Sharing what we've stolen, stealing what we shared,
            Hoping to be seated when the music stops.

We grind ourselves in the middle of things,
    The ache of endless replay in cold eyes,
        The rack of want, the cost of keep,
            The final futile act of breaking bulk.

We wind ourselves in the middle of things,
    Shouldering the shroud like a mantle of rank,
        Caressed by silken whispers
            Of a hundred hungry ghosts.

masque

unbolting slowly from the creosote pole,
the Grain Belt beer sign rasps
a halting epitaph for this sad tavern,
the yaw, a beacon tap no longer,
warning travelers of the bar
beyond the maw of evergreens,
listing, hidden like a haunted lodge.

THINGS

One Tuna Caught this Day in Diamant

"Pas des yeux!"
The withered scold
In arid voice as parched
As her wise skin
Cuts through chorales of frugal wives,
Strains to conduct
In cadence kinder to her purse,
(Mindful of unhaggled mangoes,
Okra, cane)
The dull cleaver,
Thumbs already on the scales,
To slow the beats per measure
Slapped down on her cleft fish,
Rapped smart as dominoes
On a weathered barrelhead.
Quivered gill slits seal in the sun.
Unwanted eyes cloud quickly
To their stock fate.
The bargaining beguine resumes
At the next beached boat.
His tuna parsed
Among the most insistent,
The fisher turns to
Mending nets.

THINGS

The Price of Martyrdom

This blood's for you the
      litany begins
So rich you'll never taste
      its like again
And if it isn't good
      to the last drop
You'll know you haven't got
      the real thing

THINGS

Loy Krathong

heads bowed beneath

        a full ancestral moon,
its glow diffused in this

        close humid air,
the intermarried fragrances

        of incense and exhaust
inspire among us

        awkward vigilants
an unconverted

        catalytic high
cupped in the woven palm,

        banana leaf become
a lotus boat,

        our gift begins
all life upon the klong

        a simple sacrifice this
candle, coin and flower

        to thank the river
for its petulant resistance

        for its sounding of our soul
now long possessed,

        our exorcisms fail
fouled in all manner

        by all matter
still it lifts our spirits

with our boats

Hump Flute

if i see kokopelli dance
        through one more fucking coffee shop
in one more Midwest campus town
        across a fissured plaster wall
bereft of choreography
        beyond a miles davis tape
autoreversed eternally
        I might have to foreswear caffeine
and seek serenity somewhere
        less aromatic and intense

THINGS

market music

i've felt mick
  shill for sympathy
    before first light
      in oude markt
        in Louvain
          at decibels that make
          a Belgian endive
        vendor wilt
          a ululating elvis
        mourn blue christmas
      in chautuchak
      in hot bangkok october
     threatening to distract
    the earnest dance step
   of a thai boy sweating
  to an Asian ice ice baby
in a neighboring
 stall
    the technopulse of
     akihabara
       that goads the shinjunrui
         to retroritual
           in harajuku
             before their outraged
            elders
              and hammer pound the zapotecs
            in a oaxacan zocalo
          where girls too young
         and tired to dance
       hawk chiclets
      with their marble
   rabbits
  each market
   has a music
     beyond the gold coast
      on the miracle mile
       the grounded lyric
        rhythm tone and beat
       of petty produce
       penny capital

THINGS

      locked in a jewel box
       saved in shirnkwrapped skin
     mark time until
the sale

THINGS

Hollow Ground

pro
forma
warnings,
penny rituals
be damned,
between
jimping and choil
I've carved
myself
with every blade
I've ever owned,
every edge
I've ever honed,
on the road
to damascus.

John F. Sherry, Jr. is an anthropologist who studies the sociocultural dimensions of consumer behavior and marketing. He has researched, lectured, and consulted around the globe on issues of brand strategy, experiential consumption, and retail atmospherics. He is the Raymond W. & Kenneth G. Herrick Professor of Marketing at the University of Notre Dame, and taught previously at Northwestern University's Kellogg School for over two decades. Sherry is a Fellow of the American Anthropological Association and the Society for Applied Anthropology. He is a past President of both the Association for Consumer Research and the Consumer Culture Theory Consortium, and a former Associate Editor of the *Journal of Consumer Research*. He has edited and written 10 books, authored more than 100 widely reprinted articles and chapters, published over 50 poems (including 6 co-edited chapbooks), and produced 2 videos. He is a longtime proponent of arts-based research. Sherry has won awards for his scholarly work and poetry. He is an avid flat water paddler and wilderness camper, and is still trying to perfect his seventeen foot jump shot when his five dogs allow him to share the driveway.

www.ingramcontent.com/pod-product-compliance
Lightning Source LLC
LaVergne TN
LVHW041558070426
835507LV00011B/1172